FOSTERING GRIT

How do I prepare my students for the real world?

Thomas R.
HOERR

 Alexandria, VA USA

Website: www.ascd.org   www.ascdarias.org
E-mail: books@ascd.org

Printed in the United States of America. Cover art © 2013 by ASCD. ASCD publications present a variety of viewpoints. The views expressed or implied in this book should not be interpreted as official positions of the Association.

ASCD LEARN TEACH LEAD® and ASCD ARIAS™ are trademarks owned by ASCD and may not be used without permission.

PAPERBACK ISBN: 978-1-4166-1707-5   ASCD product #SF113075
Also available as an e-book (see Books in Print for the ISBNs).

Library of Congress Cataloging-in-Publication Data
Hoerr, Thomas R., 1945-
  Fostering grit : how do I prepare my students for the real world? /
Thomas R. Hoerr.
      pages cm
  Includes bibliographical references.
  ISBN 978-1-4166-1707-5 (pbk. : alk. paper) 1. Classroom management. 2. Social skills—Study and teaching—Activity programs. 3. Life skills—Study and teaching—Activity programs. 4. Resilience (Personality trait) in children. I. Title.
  LB3013.H59 2013
  371.102′4—dc23

                                                            2013020758

21 20 19 18 17 16 15 14 13   1 2 3 4 5 6 7 8 9 10

FOSTERING GRIT

How do I prepare my students for the real world?

Want to earn a free ASCD Arias e-book?
Your opinion counts! Please take 2–3 minutes to give
us your feedback on this publication. All survey
respondents will be entered into a drawing to
win an ASCD Arias e-book.

Click here or type in this web location:
www.ascd.org/ariasfeedback

Thank you!

Why Grit?

Is our job to prepare students for success in school or for success in life? How we answer that question has powerful implications for what and how we teach. For too long, educators have focused only on getting students ready for the next test, the next grade, graduation, college, and so on. The test-score mania under which we've worked for the past decade—with students, teachers, and schools judged on percentiles—has exacerbated our short-term focus.

Don't misunderstand me: Students must be prepared to succeed in school; they must learn how to read, write, and calculate. But that's only the beginning. Our job as educators is to prepare students for success in the real world. A focus on success in life means that, beyond teaching the three *R*s, we must also teach character, emotional intelligence, responsibility, and an appreciation for the complexity of human diversity. We must also teach the virtues of *grit*—tenacity, perseverance, and the ability to never give up.

Teaching grit can be difficult for educators because the concept appears to run counter to the caring school environments that we all esteem. It is very important that students enjoy learning and want to come to school, but teaching grit necessarily means that students will experience—and perhaps embrace—some frustration and pain. We do our students no favors if we fail to prepare them for the real world because they do not know how to respond to frustration and failure. Learning how to respond positively to setbacks is essential. Regardless of their academic performance, students are bound to encounter frustrations and failures in the real world; everyone will hit the wall sooner or later. Responding appropriately when things go wrong—turning a failure into a *good* failure, one from which we learn—is key to success in life.

Executive Functions and Grit

Our executive functions regulate and monitor our ability to organize, focus, and control our experiences. Our grit helps us determine how to respond when things go wrong. Most of us have developed routines that enable us to plan, work, and be successful. Grit gives us *resilience*. It not only keeps us focused on a task but also enables us to persevere when we fail. The self-monitoring and emotional control that grit provides is an important component of our executive functioning.

Research on Grit

Here are some key resources related to grit:

- A 2011 *New York Times* article by Paul Tough titled "What If the Secret to Success Is Failure?" discusses the work of Angela Duckworth, a professor at the University of Pennsylvania who focuses on the importance of grit in an education context. (She took the term *grit* from the title of the 1969 movie *True Grit*.) Duckworth first became interested in grit when trying to understand why certain students stay in college despite facing personal hardships and difficulties. (See TEDxTalks, 2009, for a talk on grit by Duckworth.)

- Paul Tough also discusses grit in his book *How Children Succeed: Grit, Curiosity, and the Hidden Power of Character* (2012), which examines the effect of grit on students who are academically prepared for college but encounter real-world obstacles.

- My own March 2012 Principal Connection column in *Educational Leadership* is devoted to grit (see Hoerr, 2012).

- The importance of grit is indicated in a 2013 report from the U.S. Department of Education titled *Promoting Grit, Tenacity, and Perseverance: Critical Factors for Success in the 21st Century*, which expresses concern for students who are learning to "do school but are not developing the life skills to persevere in the face of challenges they will face in the real world" (p. 18). As the report notes, "Educators, administrators, policymakers, technology designers, parents, and researchers should consider how to give priority to grit, tenacity, and perseverance in curriculum, teaching practices, teacher professional development, programs, technology adoption, and out-of-school support" (p. xii). The reason for this is quite clear: "Meta-analyses of a growing body of educational research suggest that these factors can have just as strong an influence on academic performance and professional attainment as intellectual factors" (p. 1).

- In his 2008 book, *Outliers: The Story of Success*, Malcolm Gladwell notes that grit in the form of devoting at least 10,000 hours to practicing a craft or skill is essential to mastery. (He uses Bill Gates and The Beatles as examples.)
- Carol Dweck champions grit in her book *Mindset: The New Psychology of Success* (2007). Dweck believes that there are two principal modes of thinking: *fixed* mindsets and *growth* mindsets. Fixed mindsets keep intelligence static, avoid mistakes, and prioritize looking smart over learning. Because people with fixed mindsets seek situations in which success is practically guaranteed, they are unlikely to develop grit. By contrast, people with growth mindsets acknowledge that even though mistakes may not be pleasant or make things easy, they help us learn. The grit of those with growth mindsets stems from knowing that the harder they work and the longer they try, the likelier they are to succeed.

Differentiation and Grit

Just as we need to differentiate our teaching of long division, sculpture, or the Magna Carta based on students' scholastic readiness, we also need to differentiate how we teach grit based on students' *emotional* readiness. We must know what degree of frustration our students can presently accept. In the same way that we work to improve students' scholastic skills by beginning with their current proficiency level, we work to improve students' grit by beginning with their current capacity to handle obstacles.

Working to develop grit means occasionally and thoughtfully presenting students with learning obstacles that they must overcome to find success. When doing this, we should support our students by providing them with clear tasks, strategies, care, and encouragement. Consistent success is *not* the goal here; the real goal is for students to feel frustration so they can learn how to respond to it. This approach is a far cry from the usual, in which we seek to avoid frustrating students, but *teaching children how to respond to frustration and failure requires that they experience frustration and failure.*

Differentiating for grit can occur in three contexts—process, content, and product:

- **Process.** We can elicit grit in the learning process by having students learn in a way that does not come easily to them. From a multiple-intelligences perspective, this means having students use one of the intelligences that is not a strength of theirs. For example, strong writers might be asked to learn about life during the Renaissance by drawing inferences from paintings or listening to music; interpersonal and gregarious students may be asked to work individually while introverts work in teams. Limiting the time available for a task may be another way to elicit grit. How do students respond when they cannot finish? Does the experience inform their planning behavior? Can they keep from being discouraged when they did not have sufficient time?

- **Content.** Using content to help students learn grit means introducing them to levels of complexity that cause frustration. No two students are at the same learning level, so each one's frustration level will vary. We normally push students to excel, exhorting them to do better and helping them find their groove. In teaching for grit, however, we intentionally take our students out of their comfort zones. When students have successfully mastered the required content, our responsibility is to help them pursue additional, more difficult content or to have them learn in ways that are challenging to them.
- **Product.** Asking students to create a product that serves as evidence of what they have learned can be another way to elicit grit. The product can be such that students must overcome obstacles to create it—a finely crafted and revised written paper, for example, or a highly rehearsed oral presentation. How students *show* what they've learned can require determination and tenacity beyond the learning itself.

Differentiating for grit must always be done in a spirit of care and support. Because we want students to enjoy learning and see themselves as learners, we must carefully monitor how they respond to their frustrations and failures. We must clearly explain to them what is happening and why.

Once students understand the importance of grit and what it takes to learn it, they can feel safe and supported even when things aren't going right for them.

Another way to view differentiation is to think about Lev Vygotsky's zone of proximal development (ZPD). Good teachers regularly operate within a student's ZPD—that is, the point at which a student is stretched and needs external help but still has a good chance of succeeding. In teaching for grit, however, we want students to be forced to go *beyond* their ZPD—to confront frustration, and maybe even failure, before they succeed.

The Needs of High Flyers

It's no surprise that we enjoy teaching the students who volunteer correct answers, excel at extracurricular activities, and make the honor roll. These students' successes tell us that we are good teachers! Of course we feel better when the class average on a test is 93 instead of 83 or (gasp!) 63. But what learning opportunities may be lost to students when the class average is especially high?

We understand that students who go from success to success will be unprepared for life's frustrations simply because they have no knowledge of them. How can students learn what they have not experienced? Leading these "high flyers" through the frustration and failure necessary to develop grit is not easy, but it is part of their preparation for the world beyond school. Several professors at an elite university have told me how difficult it can be for freshmen who were high school valedictorians to suddenly be surrounded by fellow high achievers. When these students perform at a less-than-stellar level, their self-image is threatened. It is often the first time that these students have needed to be resilient; consequently, it's very difficult for them.

Communicating clearly with the parents of high flyers is very important. Because they're not used to their children experiencing frustration, we need to explain to them how it can actually be beneficial. We should encourage parents to praise effort over ability, just as we need to do in the classroom.

The Needs of Struggling Students

Educators who hear about the need to teach for grit typically go through a process of acceptance followed by denial. At first, they readily understand the importance of grit and appreciate its role in success. It's hard to argue with the need for students to learn how to become tenacious and respond to failure. But soon, these same educators begin to worry about their students who routinely struggle. Consciously creating obstacles for the high flyers makes sense, but don't students who struggle already have too much experience with failure? It's a fair question. Unfortunately, for too many students, success is elusive and frustration is the norm. It's reasonable to think that students with a history of failure are the ones who most need encouragement, motivation, and a positive attitude. And they do! But they also need grit. Indeed, the case can be made that struggling students need grit even more than their high-achieving peers, because they are confronted with frustration and failures on a regular basis.

Teaching for grit is much the same regardless of the student's performance level. Struggling students may need more encouragement than high flyers, but not always. Because teaching for grit is developmental, the emotional readiness of the learner should determine the teacher's approach. Struggling students may learn grit more easily in nonscholastic areas, and they may need more encouragement to succeed than high flyers. We need to support *all* learners and have them understand that, although the pursuit of grit is hard, we are exposing them to difficult experiences because we care for them.

Multiple Intelligences and Grit

Good assessments provide more than a description of what a student knows and can do; they can also serve as teaching tools from which students can learn. With good assessments, students learn about content and about themselves. The use of multiple intelligences (MI) can be particularly useful in student assessment. The MI approach is attractive partly because it provides different pathways through which students can learn. Using MI enables us to offer students learning avenues other than those associated with linguistic or logical-mathematical intelligence, thus helping more students learn more content. However, as previously noted, there are times when we can specifically require students to use a type of intelligence in which they are *not* proficient as a way of teaching them grit. This strategy can be particularly appropriate for high-performing students who are very skilled in the three *R*s, as the obstacles it places in their paths may not jeopardize their academic records.

Grit Begins with You

Because teaching for grit requires students to experience frustration and, sometimes, failure, *we must remain positive, encouraging, and hopeful*. Planning to forge ahead despite difficulties makes it more likely that students will persevere, as does expressing support for students' efforts and applauding their tenacity. Teaching for grit doesn't mean becoming a curmudgeon or giving up that special rapport with students. If we accept our roles in teaching for grit, we can still be respected and loved as long as our students (and their parents/guardians) understand the goal and strategies involved.

It's natural to ask what to do in your classroom on Monday to teach for grit, but teaching for grit is more of an attitude than a strategy. Of course, strategies are necessary to help students learn and develop grit, but the process begins with teachers and administrators accepting different responsibilities and a new, more complex role in preparing students for success. Contrary to much of our training as teachers and administrators, we need to become comfortable with *occasionally* putting students in a position where they have to struggle, show tenacity, and exhibit resilience. Teaching for grit requires a new mindset about the goals of education and our roles as educators in helping students succeed. The Teacher Grit Survey (see Figure 1) can give you a sense of how you view the place of grit in the learning process. I suggest taking it with colleagues and then comparing scores and discussing the implications.

Sharing About Grit

When I make presentations about grit to educators, I usually ask them to reflect on their personal experiences. I distribute a sheet that asks when and where they learned grit and how they use it today. I use this approach to illustrate to teachers that we all have used grit to achieve success. Asking them to reflect on their own grit and how it has contributed to their personal successes helps them become more comfortable with the importance of grit and with their role in teaching it to students. Hearing others' stories exposes them to different ways to think about grit.

Here's an example. I began our school's faculty inservice session by asking the teachers to consider which of the multiple intelligences required the most grit when they were growing up. (I asked this question because ours is an MI school.) One teacher shared a story about the paper route he had as a child. He recalled delivering papers on his bike and walking through the snow when it was the only way he could go from house to house. Though he referred to it as the "dreaded paper route," he noted that it taught him the importance of getting up and getting to work, even if it's challenging and not your favorite thing to do. Another teacher talked about how hard she worked at running when

---

FIGURE 1: **Teacher Grit Survey**

The following questions are designed to provide a sense of your receptivity to grit. Place a 1 (strongly disagree), 2 (disagree), 3 (not sure), 4 (agree), or 5 (strongly agree) after each item. This is an anecdotal test, designed simply to help you reflect on your level of personal grit and degree of comfort teaching for grit in your classroom.

1. Intellect determines success. ___
2. Students should always have chances to redo work. ___
3. Students' trajectories should help determine their grades. ___
4. My goal is happy students. ___
5. In my professional life, I often succeed because I don't give up. ___
6. In my personal life, I often succeed because I don't give up. ___
7. Students lose confidence when they fail. ___
8. When things are hard for me, I find myself being distracted. ___
9. Noncognitive skills are mostly developed outside of school. ___
10. I am comfortable sharing my mistakes and what I learn from them. ___

Scoring:

- Total points for questions 2, 3, 5, 6, 10 = A
- Total points for questions 1, 4, 7, 8, 9 = B
- Subtract B from A to find your grit score.

A score of 18 or more means you are gritting away! A score of 14–17 means you understand grit but need to work more directly on it. A score of less than 14 may mean that you need some remedial lessons in grit. If your score is under 12, review the Duckworth and Tough resources listed in the "Research on Grit" section. Don't give up if it seems difficult!

she was younger. She would ask her dad to help her, and he coached her on techniques and timed her. She went on to win races and attributes her successes to not giving up and being able to ask for help. After the teachers shared with the whole group, I had them gather in small groups to share what they had written with one another. I know that the discussions were rich because it was hard for me to regain the group's attention!

Modeling Grit

When it comes to teaching the noncognitive curriculum, one mistake educators often make is to underestimate our value as role models. Our actions speak louder than our words, and that's especially true when it comes to grit. Our students need to know that somewhere along the way—maybe *lots* of places along the way—we used grit to find our success. Our students need to know that most of us weren't "born on third base."

I understand that it can feel less than professional to talk with students about our personal experiences. This may especially be the case when it comes to sharing ways in which we've dropped the ball and had to try again. However, sharing our own vulnerabilities and examples of grit can be a powerful lesson for our students. What we've learned along the path to success might be the best thing we can teach. The more students recognize how important grit has been to people they know and respect, the better. (Note: It's important here to be particularly thoughtful about personal boundaries. Although it's helpful for students to see your grit, some personal areas should remain off limits.)

Grit and Competition

Although the recently adopted Common Core State Standards (CCSS) for English language arts and mathematics do not speak directly to the teaching of grit, they still offer support in this area. According to the official CCSS website (www.corestandards.org), "No state in the country was asked to lower their expectations for their students in adopting the Common Core. The standards are evidence-based, aligned with college and work expectations, include rigorous content and skills, and are informed by other top performing countries" (Common Core State Standards Initiative, 2012). The fact that rigorous content and skills are explicitly mentioned in the CCSS may make it more likely that students will experience the frustration and failure that are integral to learning grit.

Where did *you* learn your grit? I've asked this question a lot to parents and educators who invariably tell me that they developed their grit during extracurricular activities. Most of them say they did so learning to play sports or a musical instrument; only rarely do they attribute their grit to academic experiences.

I, too, developed my grit learning to play sports. My journey began on the football field in high school. Though I loved the game, I wasn't a particularly good player. For the first time in my life, I was pushed beyond what I thought I could handle, but I survived. I learned to pick myself up and try again when I failed. Now, decades later, that message remains with me. Although I sure didn't know it at the time, my lack of football skills may have actually benefitted me in the long run!

Extracurricular experiences offer great opportunities for students to learn grit. In sports, children are relentlessly pushed—by the coach, by teammates, sometimes by their parents—to do better and better; performances can always be improved. When you fail at athletics, you do so publicly—the pitcher's mound offers no place to hide. Of course, there are also winners and losers. Effort, improvement, and teamwork all matter, but a scoreboard publicly proclaims the victor. (One of the soccer teams at my school once played in a league that did not record goals in order to reduce competitiveness. The players kept score anyway.) Of course, our hearts go out to the children in tears after losing or in pain due to physical exertion. We would be appalled to find these things happening in our classrooms, but on the field or in the gym, they can help students learn about grit.

Of course, many of the same grit-building experiences found in sports can be found in any number of extracurricular activities, whether it's the drama club or the debate team. In all cases, these experiences have two things in common: they are public, and students are held accountable by their peers (their club or team).

The Need for Grit in Our No-Pain Culture

The need to formally teach grit is greater today than it was in the past. As parents become increasingly overprotective, they encounter fewer opportunities to expose their kids to grit-building frustration. The term *snowplow parents*—for parents who feel their job is to remove the barriers that their children might encounter—captures this attitude. Of course, parents should be their children's foremost advocates, but they aren't helping their kids by serving as a buffer between them and failure. When making the case for grit to parents, consider sharing writings that speak to the importance of perseverance. Here are a few good examples (see References for URLs):

- "Math and Science Engagement: Identifying the Processes and Psychological Theories That Underlie Successful Social-Psychological Interventions," a briefing paper by Nancy Stano (2012).
- "The Mindsets That Foster 'Productive Persistence' in Students," a blog post by Michael Keany (2013).
- "Teaching Kids to Have a Strong Work Ethic," a blog post by Michele Borba (2012).
- "Struggle for Smarts? How Eastern and Western Cultures Tackle Learning," a blog post by Alex Spiegel (2012).
- "For President, I Want the Guy Who's Failed," a blog post by Jeff Stibel (2012).
- "America Needs More Free-Range Kids: Grit Made America Great," an article by John Stossel (2013).

The Six Steps of Teaching for Grit

Regardless of content area or student age, teaching for grit requires the same six-step process. Implementation varies according to grade, subject matter, and each student's individual abilities, but the steps themselves are consistent:

1. Establish the environment.
2. Set the expectations.
3. Teach the vocabulary.
4. Create the frustration.
5. Monitor the experience.
6. Reflect and learn.

Step 1: Establish the Environment

It is very important to ensure that our students feel cared for and supported when teaching for grit. They need to be reminded that doing poorly or finding something difficult doesn't mean that we will value them any less. As my teacher friend Kristi says, "If you establish good relationships with students and approach education as a whole series of trials and errors, teaching for grit will be a moot issue."

Ask yourself how you measure success in your classroom. Beyond celebrating academic achievement, how do you acknowledge students? Do you recognize their efforts and improvements? Do you give them time to share difficulties they're having and publicly support one another? How do you choose the student work that you post on your walls and in the halls? Effort needs to be valued; hard work needs to be made cool.

When establishing an environment conducive to teaching for grit, we need to anticipate students' experiences *from our perspectives*. Is the kind of frustration students will experience going to be new to them? How will they handle it? Will their parents understand? Answering those questions should inform the strategies you will need to provide the caring and safe environment necessary to teach for grit.

Step 2: Set the Expectations

Students need to appreciate the value of struggling to succeed, and they need to learn that mistakes are lessons. In addition to charts showing how many books students have read or which students have received *A*s, consider posting a "grit chart" on which students can use symbols to record instances when they've "toughed out" a difficult task.

Students need to understand grit so they can consciously work to develop it. They must also know and be reminded that we care for them and want them to do well despite sometimes allowing them to "hit the wall." The Student Grit Survey (see Figure 2) can help students reflect on their approaches to problem solving and how they see grit. Distributing it before discussing grit increases the likelihood that students will give an objective response. Be sure to let students know that the survey is designed to help them reflect on how they approach difficulties.

FIGURE 2: **Student Grit Survey**

Answering these questions can help you understand how much grit plays a role in your learning. Place a 1 (strongly disagree), 2 (disagree), 3 (not sure), 4 (agree), or 5 (strongly agree) after each item.

1. No matter how difficult a task is, I keep trying. ___

2. I would rather practice something I do well than try to learn something new. ___

3. I am often distracted when things are hard. ___

4. Learning in school should be easy. ___

5. I usually work harder than my classmates. ___

6. It is important to me that I don't make mistakes. ___

7. I would rather get a *B* in a new area of learning than an *A* on something I already know. ___

8. Learning must be fun. ___

9. It's OK if I make a mistake or two while learning. ___

10. If something is difficult, I am sure to devote extra time to it. ___

Scoring:
- Total points for questions 1, 5, 7, 9, 10 = *A*
- Total points for questions 2, 3, 4, 6, 8 = *B*
- Subtract *B* from *A* to find your grit score.

A score of 18 or more means you've got grit! A score of 14–17 means you need to work more directly on grit. A score of less than 14 may mean that you need to try harder at trying harder. If your score is under 12, then you and your teacher should have a conversation about grit.

Step 3: Teach the Vocabulary

All students need to have the word *grit* in their working vocabulary and use it habitually in the classroom, at recess, and in the halls. One way to ensure they do this is to use the word when commenting on students' papers (e.g., "Fred, your progress shows that you're using a great deal of grit!" "Aaron, did you give this project your full effort? I don't see much grit here"). Students' parents need to understand and be comfortable with the word, too. Here are some examples of ways to incorporate *grit* in reports to parents:

- "I've been so pleased to see Sally's efforts to develop grit. She really hangs in and tries harder when things are difficult."
- "Let's discuss grit at Jose's conference. I want him to learn how to handle frustration."
- "Maurice is a good student, but he's too tentative at times. Let's talk about what we can do to help him develop grit."
- "JuJu shows lots of grit!"

We have been incorporating *grit* into everyone's vocabulary at my school—teachers, students, and parents. Here's what Nina, one of the teachers at my school, has to say about the experience:

I've been more intentional about using the term *grit* and discussing it in advisory. Sometimes students will share things from the weekend—"I lost my soccer game and was really down"—and we will talk about what it looks like to face that situation with grit and what it looks like without grit. Or I will provide scenarios: You worked hard, tried out for the basketball team, and still didn't make it. What does grit look like? Is that easy or hard for you? How do you react in that situation? Is it natural or something you consciously need to work on?

If your students are occasionally included in parent-teacher conferences, grit would be a wonderful topic for discussion. Having everyone around the table increases the likelihood that parents and educators can work together to help students develop grit.

There are other vocabulary terms that support teaching grit: *failure, frustration, tenacity, perseverance, resilience, self-confidence, self-image, comfort zone.* Administrators need to encourage the use of these terms. For example, I wrote the following in a bulletin to faculty at my school:

Comfort Zone: Have you used the term with your kids lately? Recall, please, that at my grit presentation, I talked about how we all need to move out of our comfort zones. Part of this process is explaining the term to your students and their parents. The goal is for kids to understand and be able to say something like "This is out of my comfort zone, but I'm going to try it anyway." Likewise, comfort zone is a key factor in our parent education—I am convinced. Please use it in your teaching, your classrooms, and your parent letters.

1: Create the Frustration

The frustration necessary for developing grit can some-times stem from ambiguity. If a task isn't clear or presents too many options, students may want to walk away before even beginning. It's important to be attuned to students' emotions, attitude, and confidence so you know when to intervene. Teach students to be aware enough of their own feelings to be able to anticipate frustration, allowing them to take a deep breath and forge ahead.

One way to determine whether students have internal-ized the notion of grit is by observing how readily they rec-ognize the need for it. Consider whether it's more effective to teach your students about grit before they experience a frustrating task or to use the moment when they hit the wall as a teaching opportunity.

When teaching for grit, we must take care not to jeopar-dize students' confidence or self-image. With that caveat in mind, here are a few strategies for instilling grit in students:

- Knowingly give an assignment that is out of a student's comfort zone.
- Require a student to revise and revise again until his or her work is perfect.
- Tell a student to forge ahead even if the directions are unclear.

As a principal, I normally would not want my teachers to use the above strategies. However, they can *occasionally* be used within the context of teaching for grit. Alternatively, you may want to designate a particular day as Grit Day.

This day is planned to contain frustration for students, and the goal is for them to work through it. Students and their parents should know about Grit Day ahead of time; in the weekly letter to parents, you might write something such as "Get extra sleep because next Tuesday is Grit Day." This type of proactive communication gives you license to create situations that are neither easy nor pleasant. At the end of Grit Day, you can ask students what they learned about themselves from their reactions and behaviors and how they might apply what they've learned to other tasks.

Here are some ways to keep students persevering when they hit a wall:

- Before students start on a task, ask them to anticipate how hard they think it will be. They should identify something else they've done that seems to be at the same level of difficulty.
- Ask students to think of a task at which they were successful but didn't think they would be. How did grit play a part in their success?
- Have students promise to give five solid minutes of full-force effort to the task. At the end of the five minutes, students who are excelling should continue their work, but students who are struggling should stop, take a deep breath, and reflect on what they might do differently. (Depending upon individual students' emotional readiness, they may have to stop and reflect more or less frequently than their classmates.)
- Remind students that a *good* failure is one from which they learn. What are they learning about the

task? What are they learning about their preparation and what they might do differently? What are they learning about trying harder and hanging in?

There are times when students exhibit grit but still find success elusive. In such cases, help your students realize that it's better to give your all and not succeed than to simply walk away from a challenge. Students need to understand that they are stronger simply for having tried far more than they thought possible. For older students, this may a good time to share the adage "What doesn't kill you makes you stronger." (You should definitely be prepared for the retort, "This *is* killing me!") Sadly, some students have become accustomed to giving up quickly when frustration occurs. Here, your job is to help students learn that success is possible. The term *good failure* may help them understand that. These students will probably require more intensive intervention and encouragement than their classmates.

It's possible to make learning grit interesting and even fun. For example, here's a performing arts teacher describing how he instills grit in his students:

I began the year with a unit on circus skills that included learning how to juggle and how to spin plates on sticks. Both are particularly challenging skills that can only be mastered through continuous practice. I've structured my lessons to include time for practicing specific skills ("technique time") as well as time for creative exploration ("trick time"). We've discussed grit each time as being a necessary characteristic in successful performers. We've talked about all performance skills being similar in their grit requirement. If you're going to be a great piano player, you don't get that way overnight or even in a year. You gain success through determined practice. That practice isn't always "fun," but it's necessary and valuable.

In regards to spinning plates, I had to learn this skill myself in order to teach it. It took me about one and a half hours of trial and error before my first successful spin. I must have dropped the plate 500 times. I was able to talk with the kids about my experience in order to prepare them for the fact that this was challenging but doable with persistence. I should add that there's no way for a teacher to help kids in this endeavor beyond offering directions and advice. It's just something that you have to keep trying until you finally get it.

The kids really worked hard at developing the skills. There were lots of frustrating moments handled with relative grace resulting in measurable success. The kids request the opportunity to return to juggling and spinning plates daily.

The conversations about grit have carried over into other activities. We've been working on singing in ensemble with the 5th grade, another very challenging activity where early failures must be endured, reflected upon, and overcome in order to become successful. Really, grit has been a constant topic in performing arts.

Step 5: Monitor the Experience

Because there is no formula for teaching grit, we need to be very aware of our students' individual frustration levels and how they respond to them. Sometimes, instead of putting down their pencils and declaring "I'm done," students may seem to still be working on a task when in fact they've quit emotionally; they are no longer invested in trying to succeed. Because surrendering to frustration can be so hard to perceive, it's essential to monitor students' efforts, keep them focused on the task, and prevent them from moving on to a different activity.

Often, awareness of students' frustration levels begins when we ask, "How are you feeling, and what are you learning about yourself?" If your students are having trouble, ask them, "Is this a *good failure*?" Students' answers to these questions not only tell us how they are feeling but also remind them that their attitude is the key factor in their problem solving. Here are some techniques for soliciting feedback from students:

- Either periodically or at the end of a lesson, ask students to give a thumbs up or thumbs down to show how they are feeling about the task.
- On a student grit reflection questionnaire (see Figure 3), have students select a number to indicate how frustrated they are feeling, either during or at the end of class. (A legend should be posted at the front of the

classroom to show what each number represents.) Questionnaires can be passed out at the end of the week or unit.

- Ask students how they respond to frustration, then assemble like-response affinity groups so students with similar strategies can meet periodically to share successes and ideas.

- Create a two-column checklist for each student to monitor progress on grit. Fill out one column, have the student fill out the other, and compare the responses.

FIGURE 3: **Student Grit Reflection Questionnaire**		
Frustration Level	**The Work Is . . .**	**How I'm Feeling**
1	Easy	No problem!
2	OK	I'm in good shape.
3	Hard	I'll figure it out.
4	Very difficult	I'm not sure I can succeed.
5	Too hard!	I want to quit.

Step 6: Reflect and Learn

As noted above, it's essential that students reflect on their experiences after using grit. We want them to ask themselves why they didn't give up on a given task and what they learned that will help them when they get frustrated again. Having students create a grit log or journal in which they keep track of what tasks were frustrating and how they felt about that frustration can help them refer back to their emotions and responses in the future. Depending on the school culture, students might also share their efforts toward grit on a form that is attached to their report card. Reflecting and learning is key to turning a good failure into a success.

Grit Takes a Village

None of us work in isolation; we are all part of a community, surrounded by and working with people who hold different roles. Because teaching for grit runs counter to many assumptions about teaching, it's especially important to have other stakeholders on board before beginning. The people with whom you work need to understand your thinking so they can appreciate your strategies. Here are some suggestions to help spread the word about teaching grit.

Colleagues

- Start an optional book or journal group focused on grit. Paul Tough's *How Children Succeed: Grit, Curiosity, and the Hidden Power of Character* (2012) is a logical choice. Two other books that come to mind are *Unbroken: A World War II Story of Survival, Resilience, and Redemption*, by Laura Hillenbrand (2010), and *The Rebellious Life of Mrs. Rosa Parks*, by Jeanne Theoharis (2013). Each one offers many wonderful examples of grit. Excerpts from

Howard Gardner's *Frames Of Mind* (1983) and Daniel Goleman's *Emotional Intelligence* (1995) also speak to the value of grit. It might also be fun to read Susan Cain's *Quiet: The Power of Introverts in a World That Can't Stop Talking* (2012) and look for any implications that personality type may hold for grit.

- Identify a colleague or two with whom you can share your progress teaching for grit. Meeting every week or two can be a good way to reinforce the importance of grit and to share ideas.

- Periodically share strategies for teaching for grit at faculty meetings. At my school, we often share what we're doing to help our students develop grit and examples of how they display it. It is interesting to see how the strategies and examples differ between homeroom teachers and teachers of specialty subjects.

Parents and the Community

- Talk about grit at your school's fall open house. I do this, and the parent response is always very positive. I ask parents to think about the role that grit plays in their lives and to share with a person sitting nearby.

- Have a "parent grit night" designed to explain your school's approach to teaching for grit and how parents can support this at home. You might begin the meeting by asking local citizens to share how important grit has been to them, followed by a panel of the school's educators discussing how they plan to teach for grit.

- Discuss the importance of grit and your strategies for eliciting it in weekly parent letters and class notes.
- Incorporate references to effort, in general, and grit, specifically, in students' report cards.

Administrators

- Develop, through collegial discussions with administrators at your school, a common understanding of the value of grit and the strategies you will use to teach it.
- Suggest to your principal that your professional goals include some aspect of teaching for grit.

I strongly encourage principals to ask teachers what they are doing to support grit in their classrooms. I've frequently done this via faculty bulletins and faculty meetings. Here's a response I received from one of my teachers:

We read the book *Giraffes Can't Dance*, which tells the story of a giraffe who is teased for being so awkward on the dance floor. It turns out that the giraffe just needed to find the right music, and then he could dance with the best of them. Our discussions focused on no put-downs (of course), but also on not giving up just because something is challenging. We also read *Mirette on the High Wire*, which tells the story of a young girl and an experienced tightrope walker working together to overcome fear and worry and master the tightrope. We discussed how Mirette did not give up, and neither did her tightrope walker, even though they faced challenges. One of my students had a new baby sister born this year, and the transition had some challenging moments. The students shared with one another what makes being a brother or sister both fun and difficult. We also talked about other things that are hard but challenging, like learning how to play and practicing the violin, or learning the rules of soccer, or learning how to ice skate, and the importance of not giving up even though it is tough.

Halls and Walls

We should use the halls and walls of our schools to educate, not just decorate. We should display students' work, of course, and celebrate their accomplishments, but we need to go beyond simply posting the names of students on the honor roll, papers that receive an *A*, and photos of championship winners. Our halls and walls need to applaud effort, determination, and grit. Consider incorporating the following ideas on a special grit-focused bulletin board:

- Create a poster with the heading "I showed grit when I . . ." and have students complete the sentence. They may also include drawings or photos to accompany their words.

- Join with fellow educators to select students who have succeeded at a task through grit. This offers the added benefit of keeping grit in the minds of staff.
- Post (or have students post) newspaper or magazine clippings that speak to grit. These might be selected and clipped as part of a class discussion.

In addition to the above ideas, athletic coaches or club sponsors might also celebrate their grittiest players or club members by posting their names to the communal grit-focused bulletin board. Word of mouth has great power, so anything that facilitates student and staff discussions of grit is a good thing. Ideally, the bulletin board should be in a prominent and accessible space, and parents should also be encouraged to share grit successes. The goal is for grit to become part of the school community dialogue.

Teaching for Grit: A Lesson Plan

The following lesson plan is targeted to middle school students, but it can be modified for students in other grades.

Grit: The What and Why

Materials

Pictures or slides of famous individuals who have demonstrated grit.

Objectives

1. To introduce students to the concept of grit.

2. To help students identify famous people who have demonstrated grit.

3. To help students understand the role that grit will play in their success.

Anticipatory Set

1. Ask, "Does success always come easily and quickly? How do you respond when things are new or difficult?"

2. For younger students, you might initially define grit as "working harder when things are hard." Be sure to use the word *grit* regardless of the students' age.

3. Ask, "What is a 'good failure'?"

4. Explain to students that making old mistakes over again isn't good, but neither is making no mistakes at all. Mistakes are inevitable as we learn and try new things; the key is to learn from them.

Introduction

1. Explain that success doesn't only come from doing things at which we excel; it also comes from not being discouraged, not giving up, and trying again and again. By using grit, we can become good at the things that were initially hard for us.

2. Inform students that we often see the accomplishments of famous people without knowing how hard they struggled to get there. For example, Michael Jordan was cut from his high school basketball team. "I've missed more than 9,000

shots in my career," he's said. "I've lost almost 300 games. Twenty-six times I've been trusted to take the game-winning shot and missed. I've failed over and over and over again in my life. And that is why I succeed" (JayMJ3, 2006). Similarly, Abraham Lincoln was defeated in his 1832 campaign for the Illinois state legislature, his 1838 campaign for speaker of the state house, and his 1843 campaign for nomination to the U.S. House of Representatives. Though he was elected to Congress in 1846, he was not reelected in 1848, and he was defeated in his 1854 campaign for Senate, his 1856 campaign for the vice-presidential nomination, and his 1858 campaign for Senate—all before he became president. Ask your students, "Were you surprised at this? What do you think Michael Jordan and Abraham Lincoln did to keep from quitting?" Students could be assigned to identify other famous people who have demonstrated grit.

Procedures

1. Ask students if they can think of other terms for grit.

2. Use concentric circles to demonstrate the concept of a comfort zone, with inner circles containing skills within our comfort zones and outer circles indicating skills outside our comfort zones. Consider doing an initial illustration showing skills inside and outside your own comfort zone, then asking students to reflect on it.

3. Share how some skills are now in your comfort zone because you used grit to master them.

4. Ask, "What activities are currently within your comfort zone?"

5. Explain to students that failures are learning opportunities; we should learn from our mistakes.

6. Share an occasion when you displayed grit. Your candor will have a powerful effect on the class dialogue.

Assessment

Students should be able to answer the following questions appropriately:

1. Can you identify famous people who exhibit grit? How do you know they exhibit it?

2. Reflect on times when you've exhibited grit or seen someone who has. When might people want to share how they've needed grit to excel, and when might they want to appear as if they don't need it?

3. Looking ahead, on what tasks might you need to exhibit grit?

4. What behaviors or practices do you use to persevere when you're frustrated?

For older students, consider asking the following questions:

1. How do most people react when they fail and fail again? Why is that?

2. Do levels of grit vary according to socioeconomic status?

3. What role does culture play in instilling and fostering grit?

4. Would employers want to hire applicants who have grit? If so, how can you convey grit when applying for a job?

5. How can you convey grit when applying to college?

6. How would you teach younger children about grit?

Troubleshooting

As with many important goals, it is much easier to talk about developing grit than to actually do it. It is clear that children experiencing frustration and failure runs counter to our expectations. We want our students to succeed and like us; parents want their children to succeed and enjoy school. Pursuing grit in the classroom—developing students' grit so they can bounce back from failures and frustrations—causes pain. For this reason, it is essential to establish a context for grit. This means educating fellow teachers and administrators about the concept. Students' parents must be on board, too. Here's what I said in my weekly parent letter last year:

> We work to prepare students to succeed in life, not just in school. Success in school is definitely important, but it's only the floor, not the ceiling. *An important part of preparing for success in the real world is teaching students how to respond to frustration and failure.* After all, when you think about it, what's the likelihood, really, that even our most talented student is always going to succeed?
>
> We have some remarkably talented kids, and occasionally they're so skilled that they never encounter failure; they never hit the wall. Or maybe, like adults often do, they position themselves so that

they avoid the arenas where they have weaknesses. In any case, the result is the same: they are so used to doing well that they aren't well-prepared to handle that setback when it occurs.

This is a tougher issue than it might appear to be. After all, every child wants to do well, and every parent wants his or her child to excel. Sometimes kids have such a track record of success that a parent can get upset if there's a dip. Teachers often derive satisfaction and measure their effectiveness by how well their students perform. This all makes sense! And yet it all pushes against the need to create situations in which students must respond to failure by taking risks, trying harder, and being resilient.

You can read more about the ideas expressed above in Heidi Grant Halvorson's blog post, "The Trouble With Bright Kids" (2011; see References for URL).

Students must be partners in the quest for grit. They need to know what grit is and why it's important, and they need to understand that developing grit is going to be hard and sometimes unpleasant. For our part, we should view teaching for grit as another kind of differentiation. Just as we differentiate our approach to students' academic work based on their abilities and needs, we should also develop and support their grit based on their emotional needs and readiness.

Ending our overview of teaching for grit on a positive note is very appropriate. Remember that, regardless of their academic success, *all students need support, encouragement, trust, and care.* This is especially true when students are experiencing the pain or frustration of learning grit. Students should enjoy learning, and they should want to come to school. If done correctly, teaching for grit need not work against this ideal. Indeed, students who have grit will be happier at school because they will be more successful.

To give your feedback on this publication and
be entered into a drawing for a free ASCD
Arias e-book, click here or type in this
web location: **www.ascd.org/ariasfeedback**

ASCD | arias™

ENCORE

THE GRIT ALPHABET

A **Attitude** is the key. Fostering grit means viewing both student success and your role as an educator in a new way. Your goal is no longer to create a smooth slope for learning but to prepare students to succeed in the real world.

B **Beware** of fostering grit in a way that makes you seem mean, rigid, or uncaring. Students must understand that your high expectations and demanding approach stem from your concern for their success.

C **Celebrating** *how* we learn, not just *what* we learn, is important in teaching for grit. We need to celebrate students' tenacity and applaud their effort. Together, we embrace difficulty knowing that grit is the goal.

D **Dweck's** mindsets tie in very well with the pursuit of grit. Beginning in middle school, you can introduce students to Dweck's model as a way to examine the role of grit.

E **Excellence** does not mean perfection; rather, it means never giving in, never giving up, and ultimately achieving the goal.

F **Failure** is something we will all face, and fostering for grit prepares us for it. Our grit determines how we will respond when we drop the ball, hit the wall, or crash through the ice.

G **Good failures** should be embraced. No one wants to fail, and failure should be avoided, but when it happens—and it *will* happen—our goal should be to learn from it.

H **High fives**, smiling faces, and rounds of applause all play a role in helping students and their parents see that effort, trajectory, and tenacity are highly valued.

I **Intrapersonal intelligence** plays a key role in fostering grit. Students need to know how they are feeling, how they respond to adversity, and what they can do to keep on pushing.

J **"Just between us,"** says the teacher to the student, "I know you want to quit, but I also know that you can do better if you just keep trying harder." Grit is best taught through personal relationships.

K **Kindness** plays an important role in fostering grit. Students must know that their teachers and principals care for them.

L **Laughter** should be part of every lesson, and part of fostering grit is helping students learn to laugh at their mistakes. Though it may not take away the pain, laughter means that students understand that mistakes are part of learning.

M **Make new mistakes**. Students should try not to repeat errors, but they should try new things even though they know they'll make mistakes. "Make new mistakes" is a short-hand phrase you can use to help students understand that we should not fear committing errors when learning new concepts or skills.

N **Negativism** has no role in fostering grit. Even when students are pushed beyond where they think they can go, even when they are frustrated or failing, teachers and principals need to be supportive and positive about their students' efforts.

O *Occasionally* is a key word when thinking about fostering grit. Students need to face situations that we know will frustrate them, but only *occasionally*—otherwise the process becomes counterproductive and unhealthy.

P **Parents** must be on board as you pursue teaching for grit. The time you spend educating them about how their children will benefit from developing grit is an investment.

Q *Quickly* is not a word often associated with grit. By definition, grit doesn't come from easy victories or instant solutions. Students, particularly those who are usually fast learners, need to understand this.

R **Rapunzel** showed grit by waiting and waiting for her hair to grow longer and longer. An important part of grit is not always seeking easy solutions and recognizing that some important victories require time, practice, more time, and more practice.

S (Common Core) **State Standards** can help you teach for grit, as they can spark ideas for challenging your students as they learn.

T **Tenacity** is another way of describing grit.

U **Understanding** why grit is important and the process that is necessary to gain it is essential for students.

V **Vocabulary** is an important part of teaching for grit. Students need to know different ways to describe grit and how to pursue it.

W **Willingly** taking risks, trying extra-hard problems, and accepting challenges with little chance of immediate success are behaviors that occur more frequently when students have grit.

X "**X** marks the spot at the end of your comfort zone, where you feel safe," you say to a student. You then talk with the student to plan how to take risks and try new things, knowing that he or she is probably going to make mistakes.

Y "**Yes, I can!**"—an optimistic attitude that comes from grit. Students are not intimidated by failing because they know they will learn from it and will improve by trying again and again.

Z (Comfort) **Zone**—get out of it! Gaining grit doesn't come without taking risks and experiencing some pain.

References

Andrea, G., & Parker-Rees, G. (1999). *Giraffes can't dance.* London: Orchard.

Borba, M. (2012, December 13). Teaching kids to have a strong work ethic [Blog post]. Retrieved from www.micheleborba.com/blog/2012/12/13/michele-borba-blog-simple-solutions-that-teach-kids-to-persevere/

Cain, S. (2012). *Quiet: The power of introverts in a world that can't stop talking.* New York: Random House.

Common Core Sate Standards Initiative. (2012). Frequently asked questions. Retrieved from www.corestandards.org/resources/frequently-asked-questions

Dweck, C. (2007). *Mindset: The new psychology of success.* New York: Random House.

Gardner, H. (1983). *Frames of mind: The theory of multiple intelligences.* New York: Basic Books.

Gladwell, M. (2008). *Outliers: The story of success.* New York: Little, Brown.

Goleman, D. (1995). *Emotional intelligence.* New York: Bantam.

Halvorson, H. (2011, November 21). The trouble with bright kids [Blog post]. Retrieved from http://blogs.hbr.org/cs/2011/11/the_trouble_with_bright_kids.html

Hillenbrand, L. (2010). *Unbroken: A World War II story of survival, resilience, and redemption.* New York: Random House.

Hoerr, T. (2012). Got grit? *Educational Leadership, 69*(6), 84–85.

JayMJ3. (August 25, 2006). *Failure* [Video file]. Retrieved from www.youtube.com/watch?v=45mMioJ5szc

Keany, M. (2013, February 18). The mindsets that foster productive persistence in students [Blog post]. Retrieved from www.schoolleadership20.com/forum/topics/the-mindsets-that-foster-productive-persistence-in-students

McCully. E. (1992). *Mirette on the high wire.* New York: G. P. Putnam and Sons.

Spiegel, A. (2012, November 12). Struggle for smarts? How Eastern and Western cultures tackle learning [Blog post]. Retrieved from www.npr.org/blogs/health/2012/11/12/164793058/struggle-for-smarts-how-eastern-and-western-cultures-tackle-learning

Stano, N. (2012). *Math and science engagement: Identifying the processes and psychological theories that underlie successful social-psychological interventions* [Briefing paper]. Palo Alto, CA: Noyce Foundation.

Stibel, J. (2012, August 16). For president, I want the guy who's failed [Blog post]. Retrieved from http://blogs.hbr.org/cs/2012/08/for_president_i_want_the_guy_w.html

Stossel, J. (2013, May 15). America needs more free-range kids: Grit made America great [Blog post]. Retrieved from http://reason.com/archives/2013/05/15/america-needs-more-free-range-kids

TEDxTalks. (November 12, 2009). *True grit: Can perseverance be taught?* [Video file]. Retrieved from www.youtube.com/watch?v=qaeFnxSfSC4

Theoharis, J. (2013). *The rebellious life of Mrs. Rosa Parks.* Boston: Beacon.

Tough, P. (2012). *How children succeed: Grit, curiosity, and the hidden power of character.* Boston: Houghton Mifflin Harcourt.

Tough, P. (2011, September 18). What if the secret to success is failure? *New York Times,* p. MM38.

U.S. Department of Education. (2013). *Promoting grit, tenacity, and perseverance: Critical factors for success in the 21st century.* Washington, DC: Author.

Related Resources

At the time of publication, the following ASCD resources were available (ASCD stock numbers appear in parentheses). For up-to-date information about ASCD resources, go to www.ascd.org. You can search the complete archives of Educational Leadership at http://www.ascd.org/el.

ASCD EDge®

Exchange ideas and connect with other educators interested in grit and perseverance on the social networking site ASCD EDge at http://ascdedge.ascd.org/

Print Products

Activating and Engaging Habits of Mind by Arthur L. Costa and Bena Kallick (#100033S25)

Everyday Engagement: Making Students and Parents Your Partners in Learning by Katy Ridnouer (#109009)

Inspiring the Best in Students by Jonathan Erwin (#110006)

The Motivated Student: Unlocking the Enthusiasm for Learning by Bob Sullo (#109028)

ASCD PD Online® Courses

The Brain: Developing Lifelong Learning Habits, 2nd Edition (#PD11OC136)

Understanding Student Motivation Challenges (#PD09OC77)

For more information: send e-mail to member@ascd.org; call 1-800-933-2723 or 703-578-9600, press 2; send a fax to 703-575-5400; or write to Information Services, ASCD, 1703 N. Beauregard St., Alexandria, VA 22311-1714 USA.

About the Author

Thomas R. Hoerr has been the head of New City School in St. Louis, Missouri, since 1981. He has written three books—*Becoming a Multiple Intelligences School* (2000), *The Art of School Leadership* (2005), and *School Leadership for the Future* (2009)—and more than 90 articles. Readers who would like to continue the dialogue may contact Tom at trhoerr@newcityschool.org.